MazeWorld

ILLUSTRATED BY **MARK WALKER**

TEXT BY **PAUL VIRR**

ARCTURUS

ARCTURUS

This edition published in 2018 by Arcturus Publishing Limited
26/27 Bickels Yard, 151–153 Bermondsey Street,
London SE1 3HA

ISBN: 978-1-78828-517-9
CH006231NT
Supplier 29, Date 0818, Print run 7740

Text by Paul Virr
Illustrated by Mark Walker
Designed by WildPixel Ltd.
Edited by Sebastian Rydberg

Printed in China

WELCOME TO MazeWorld

To solve these mind-blowing mazes,
follow the instructions on each page.

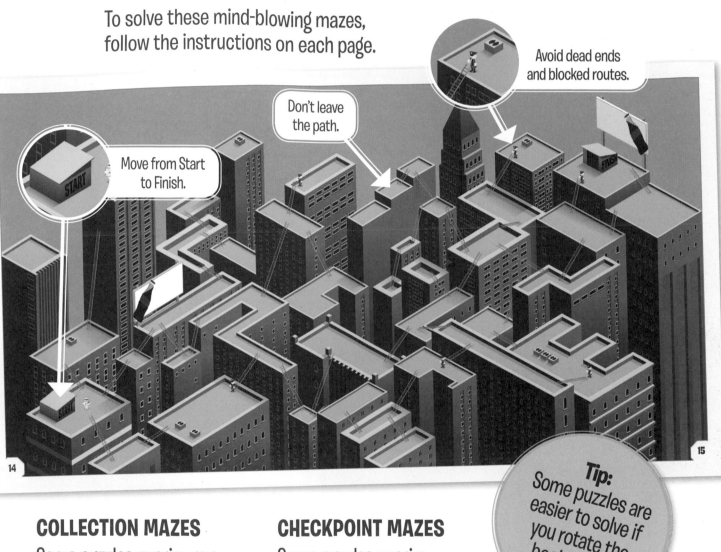

Avoid dead ends
and blocked routes.

Don't leave
the path.

Move from Start
to Finish.

Tip:
Some puzzles are
easier to solve if
you rotate the
book slightly.

COLLECTION MAZES

Some puzzles require you
to collect an object before
leaving. After collecting it,
you may need to backtrack
to get to the main path.

CHECKPOINT MAZES

Some puzzles require
you to visit a series of
checkpoints in a particular
order. It's fine to retrace
your steps.

And if you're really stuck, you can always turn to **page 88** for the solutions.

HIGH FLYER

Steer through the clouds to make a safe landing.

START

FINISH

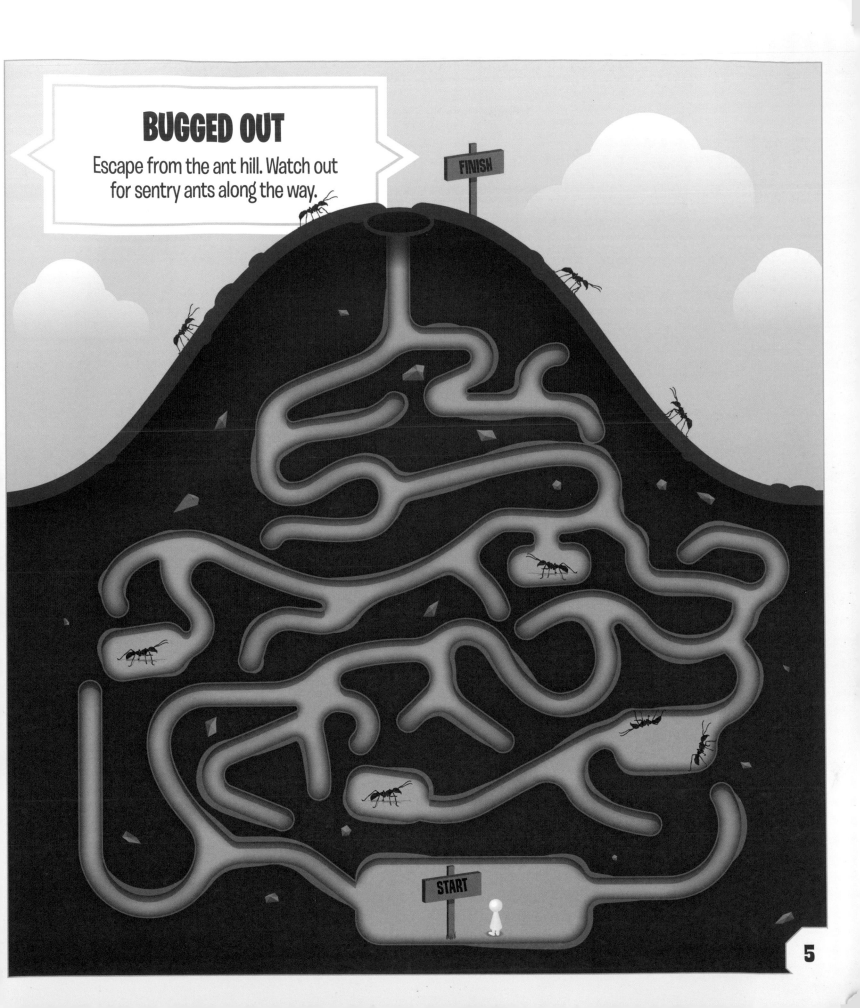

BUGGED OUT

Escape from the ant hill. Watch out for sentry ants along the way.

FINISH

START

TREETOP TRAIL

Make your way to the tree house. Avoid the monkeys, who'll swipe your lunch.

FINISH

START

CRAZY CUBES

Find a way through this eye-boggling maze, following the red route. Be sure to steer clear of hungry monsters!

START

FINISH

8

PALACE PUZZLE

Find a way through the palace garden to get to the ball.

FINISH

START

THE SERPENTS' STONE

Find the serpent that will lead you to your sailing ship.

START

FINISH

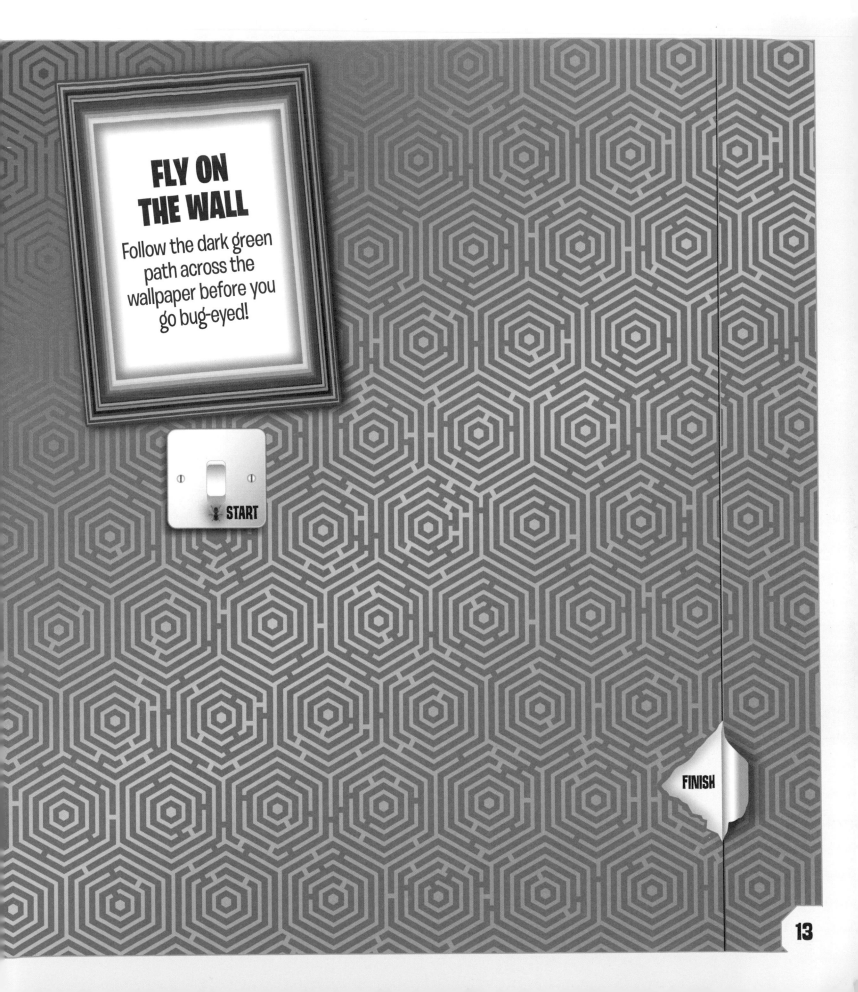

FLY ON THE WALL

Follow the dark green path across the wallpaper before you go bug-eyed!

START

FINISH

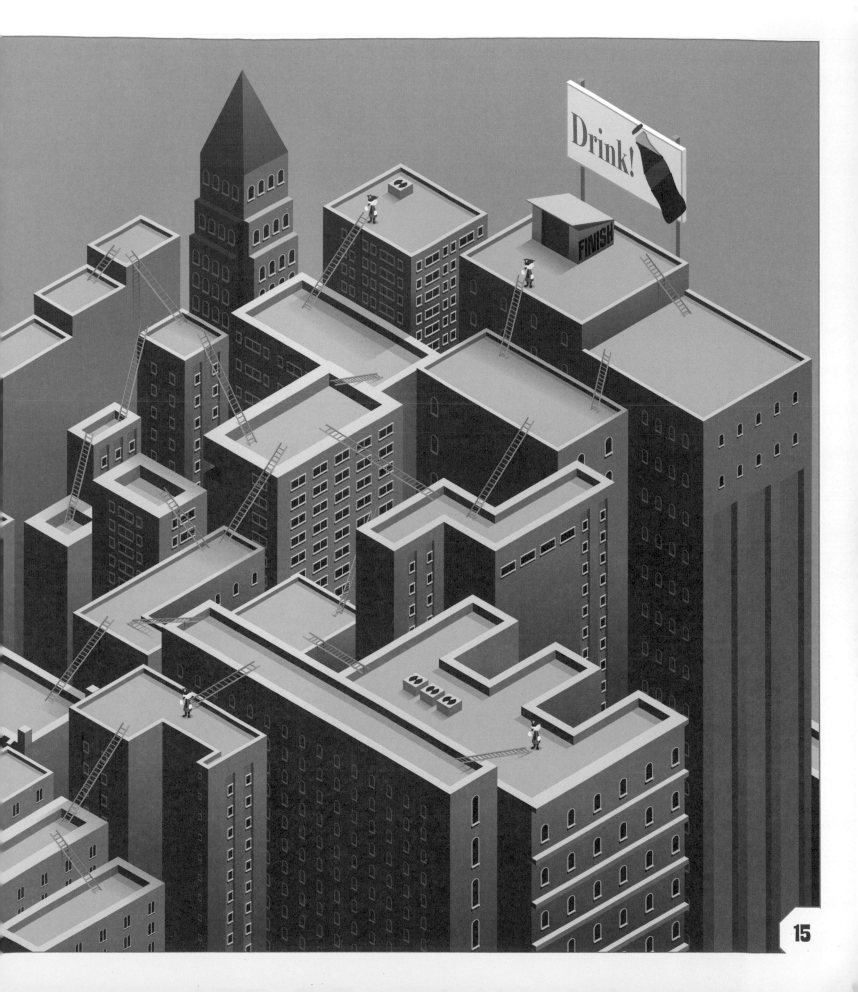

PUZZLING PIPES

Which wheel should the plumber turn to fix that leaky faucet?

A

B

C

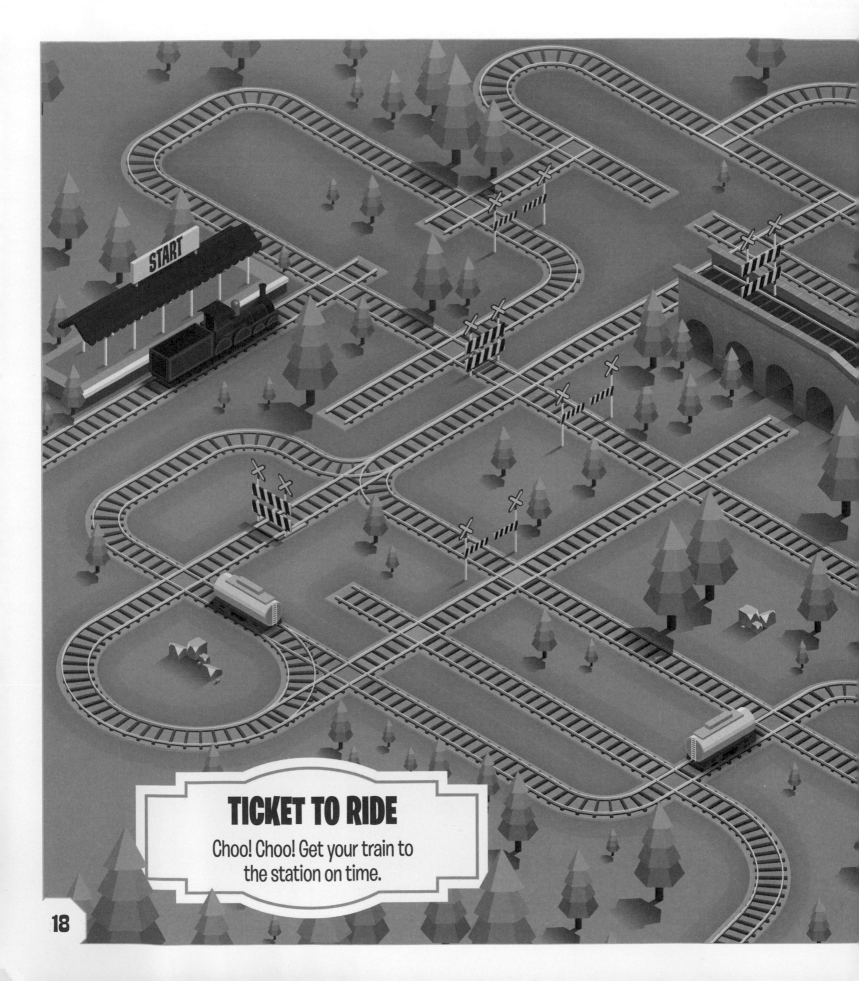

TICKET TO RIDE

Choo! Choo! Get your train to the station on time.

START

18

ON THE BEACH

Cool off with a swim—if you can find your way to the sea! Don't tread on any towels or sandcastles!

START

FINISH

DIAMONDS ARE FOREVER

If light can find a way across this sparkling diamond, so can you!

START

FINISH

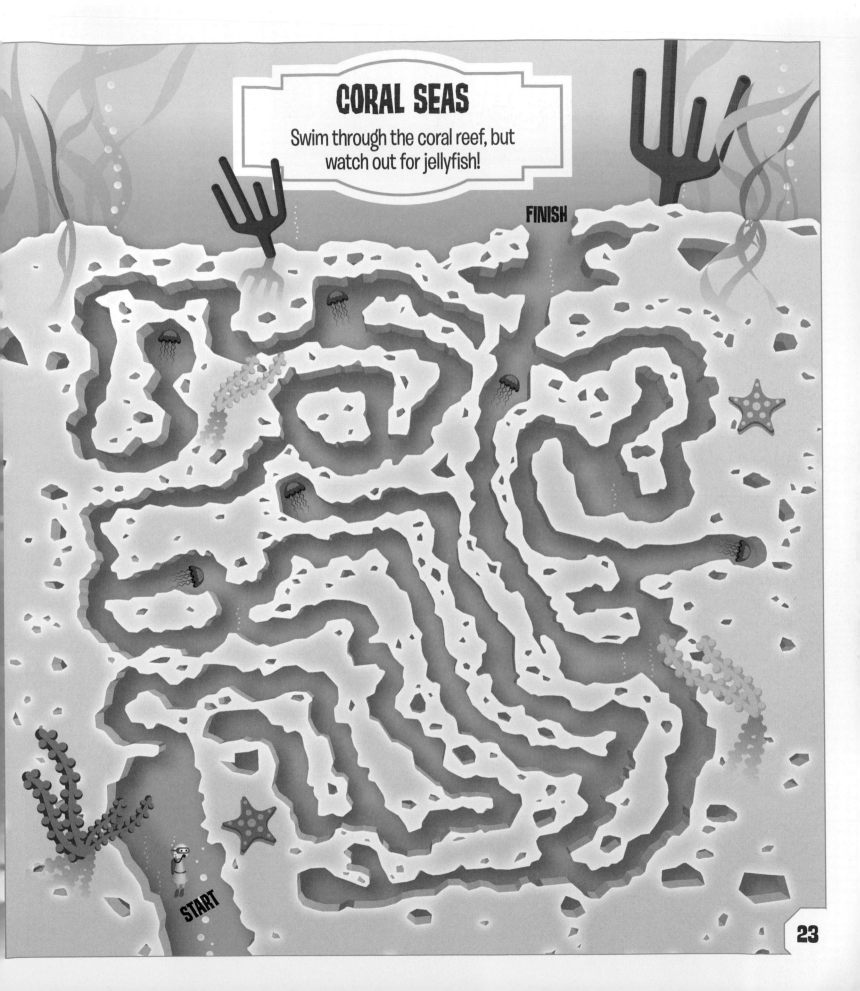

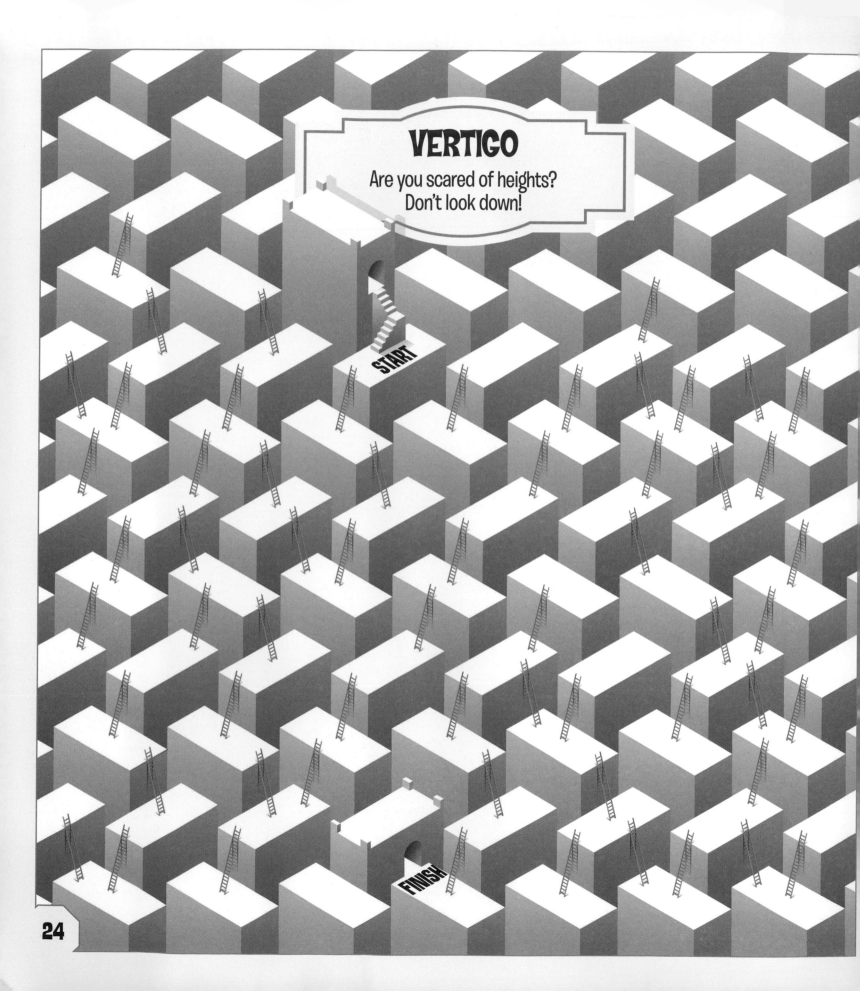

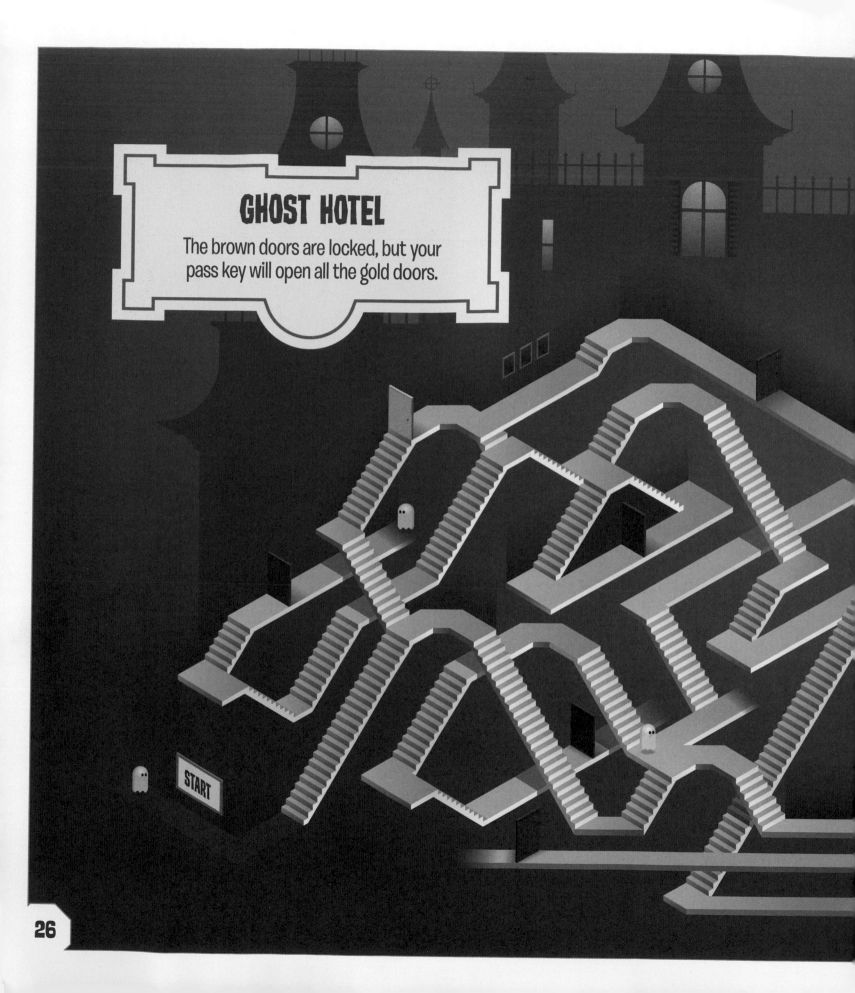

GHOST HOTEL

The brown doors are locked, but your pass key will open all the gold doors.

START

FINISH

MYSTERY MOON

Journey to a strange new world,
but try not to get lost in space.

FINISH

START

OVER THE FIELD

There is a way across the field,
but can you find it?

FINISH

START

HIGHWAY ESCAPE

It's time to get out of the city. Hit the highway, and watch out for traffic.

START

FINISH

31

THE SECRET GARDEN

Find your way to the heart
of the hedge maze.

FINISH

START

TALL ARE THE TOWERS

Sometimes you have to go up before you can get down. Mind your step on the bridge!

START

FINISH

THE BLUE LAGOON

Night is falling. Row your boat home,
but steer clear of the rocks.

START

FINISH

NIGHT HOTEL

There are plenty of doorways,
but where is the exit?

FINISH

START

37

FINISH

39

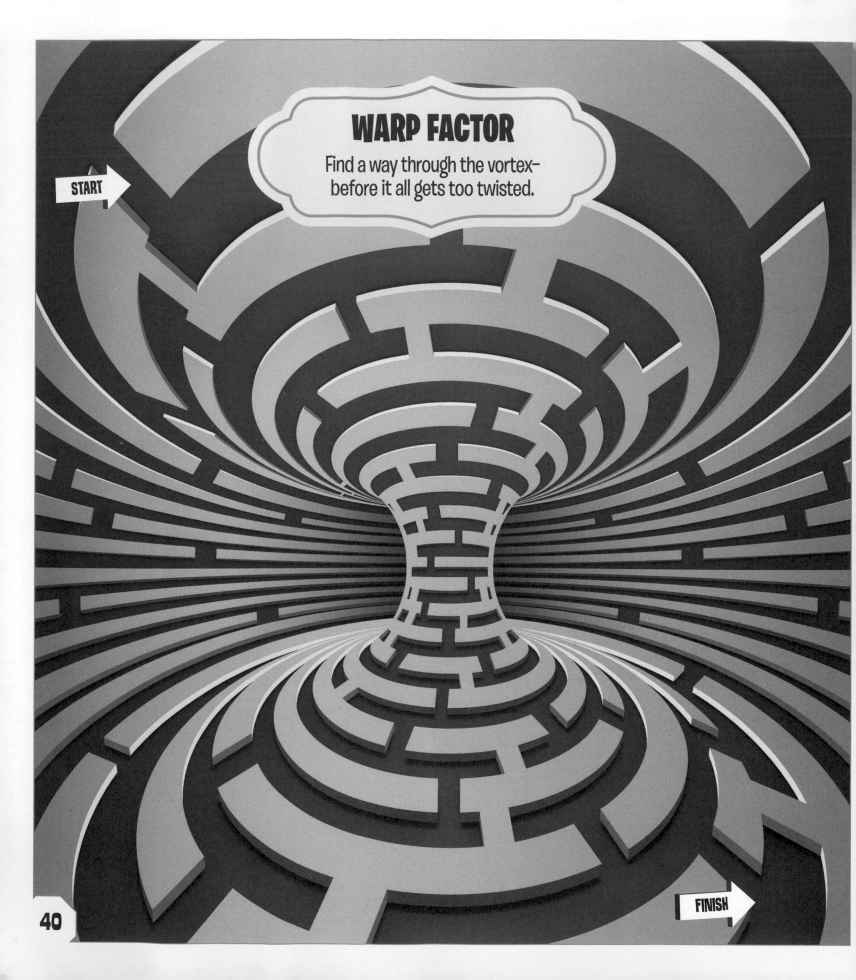

TEMPLE OF THE SUN

Climb the temple at sunrise, and you will see the light. Tread carefully, avoiding the scorpions and rock piles!

FINISH

START

THE CRYSTAL LABYRINTH

There is treasure at the end of the trail—
if you can find your way!

START

FINISH

HAVING A BALL

You'll need to use all your strength
and skill to roll the globe home.

START

FINISH

45

THE FOUNTAIN

The Fountain of Truth is in the Garden of Infinity. Seek it out!

FINISH

START

EXIT THE DRAGON

The dragon is stirring. Grab the treasure and leave... NOW!

START

GONDOLA SKIES

Take a gondola tour of the sky-high canals,
avoiding the monsters and other gondolas.

FINISH

FINISH

START

THE ASCENT

It's a long way up to the Maze of the Skull—and a long way down!

GAME OVER

This machine is in meltdown.
Time to get out of the game!

FINISH

START

PARKING SPACE

Park your car. There's a space
reserved for you—over there.

START

FINISH

53

THE HIVE

What's the buzz? Is it time to leave the beehive?

FINISH

START

CASTLE ROCK

To find the Golden Star, you'll need a head for heights.

FINISH

START

START

3

2

TO THE LIGHTHOUSES

Bring light to the lofty lighthouses, from one to four in turn.

FINISH

SCREEN TIME

Find your seat! The movie is about to begin.
Don't tread on noisy popcorn!

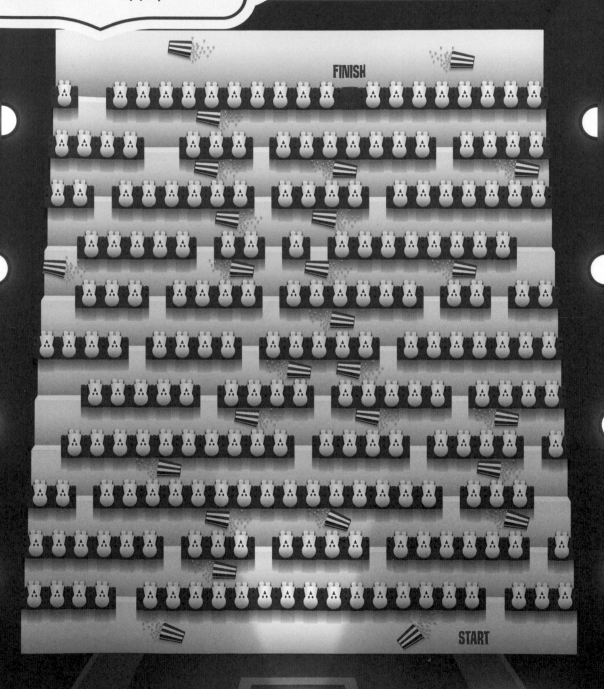

FINISH

START

INSIDE TIME

Tick. Tock. It's easy to lose track of time, but don't lose your way!

START

FINISH

RUNAWAY TRAIN

This train can't stop! Can you steer it to safety until it runs out of steam?

START

THE AMULET

Find the path that will unlock the magical powers of the amulet.

START

FINISH

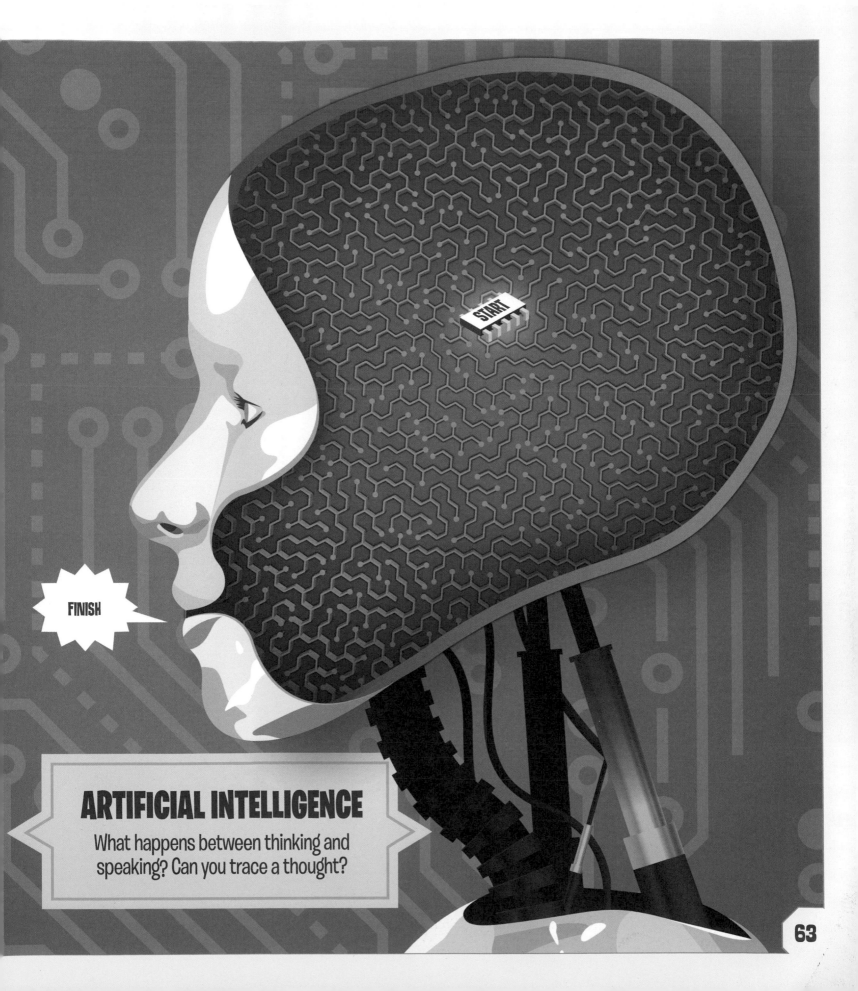

START

ABOVE THE CLOUDS

The golden chalice is yours for the taking, if you can find it!

FINISH

THE SPIRE

Time to add the finishing touch to the top of the tower. Watch your step!

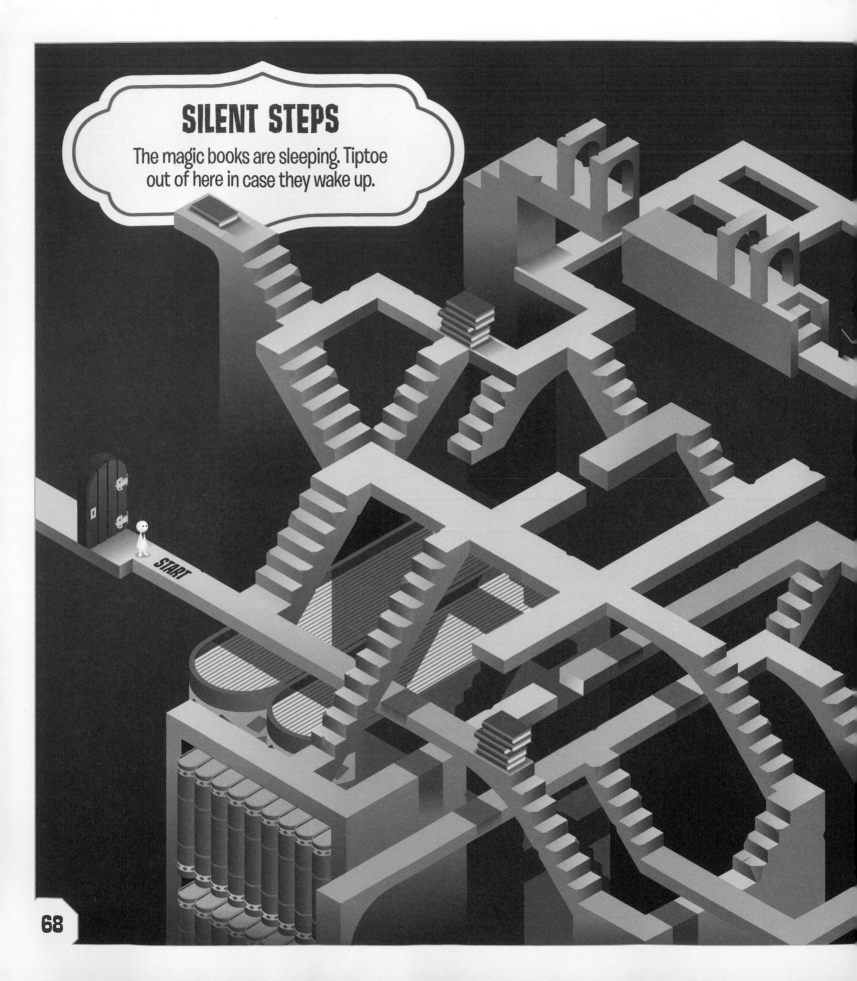

SILENT STEPS

The magic books are sleeping. Tiptoe out of here in case they wake up.

START

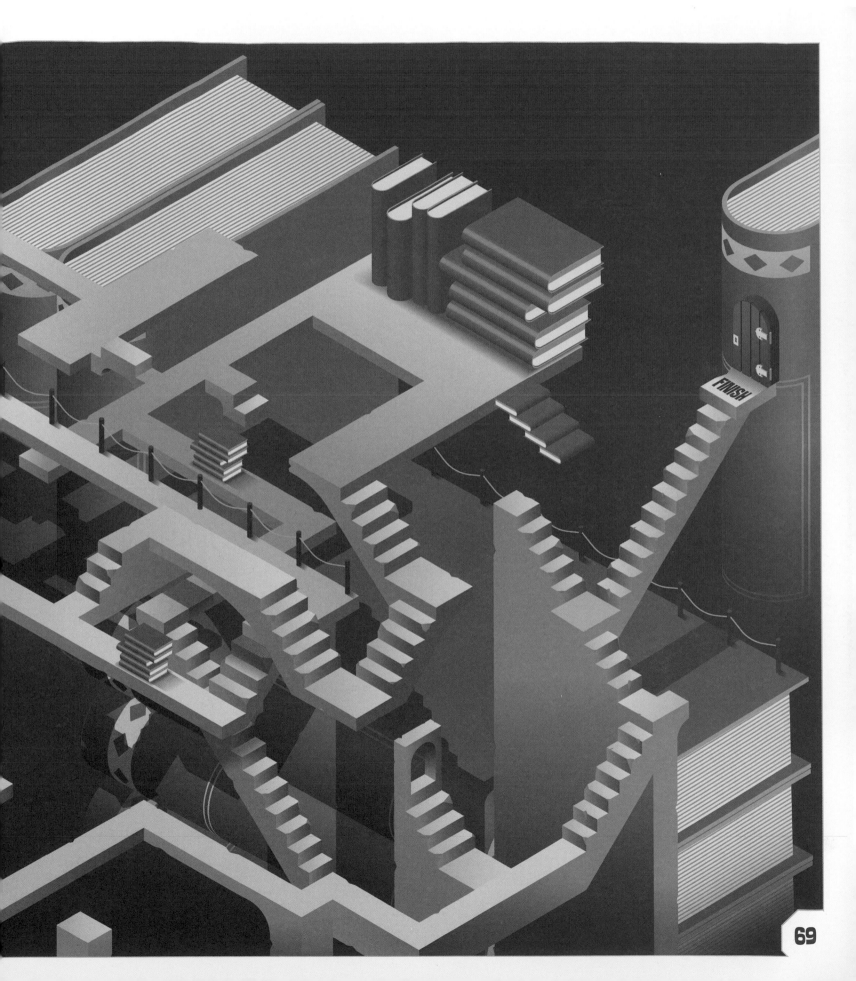

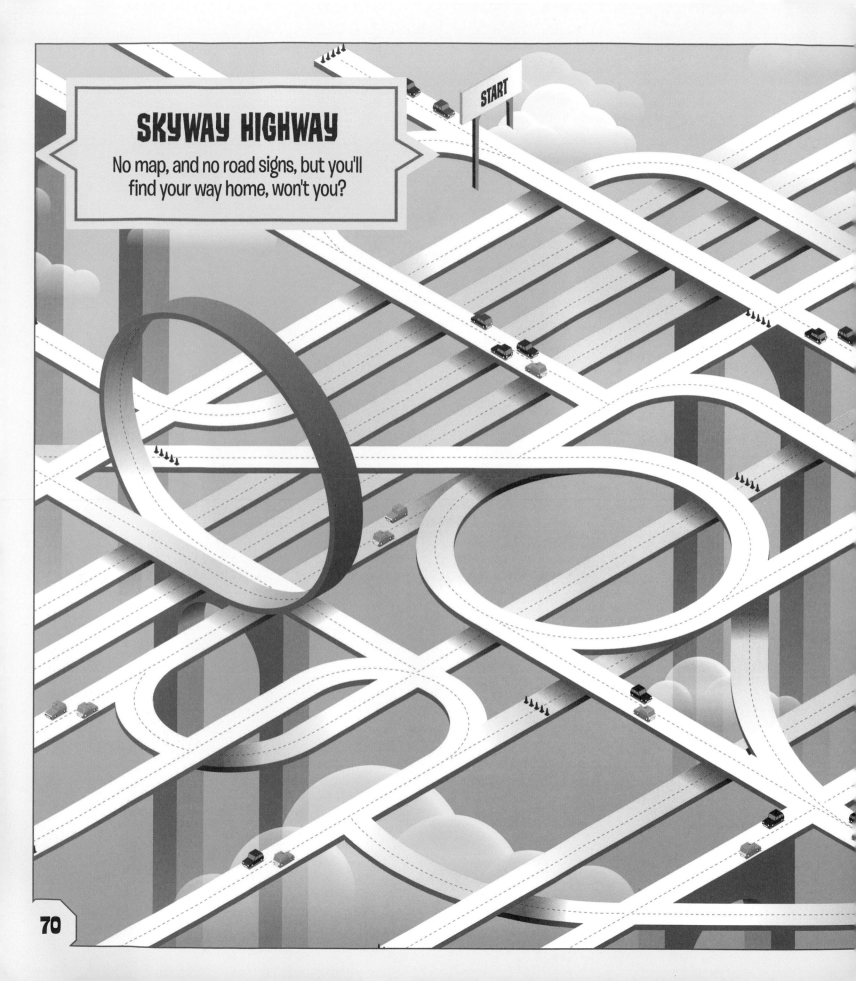

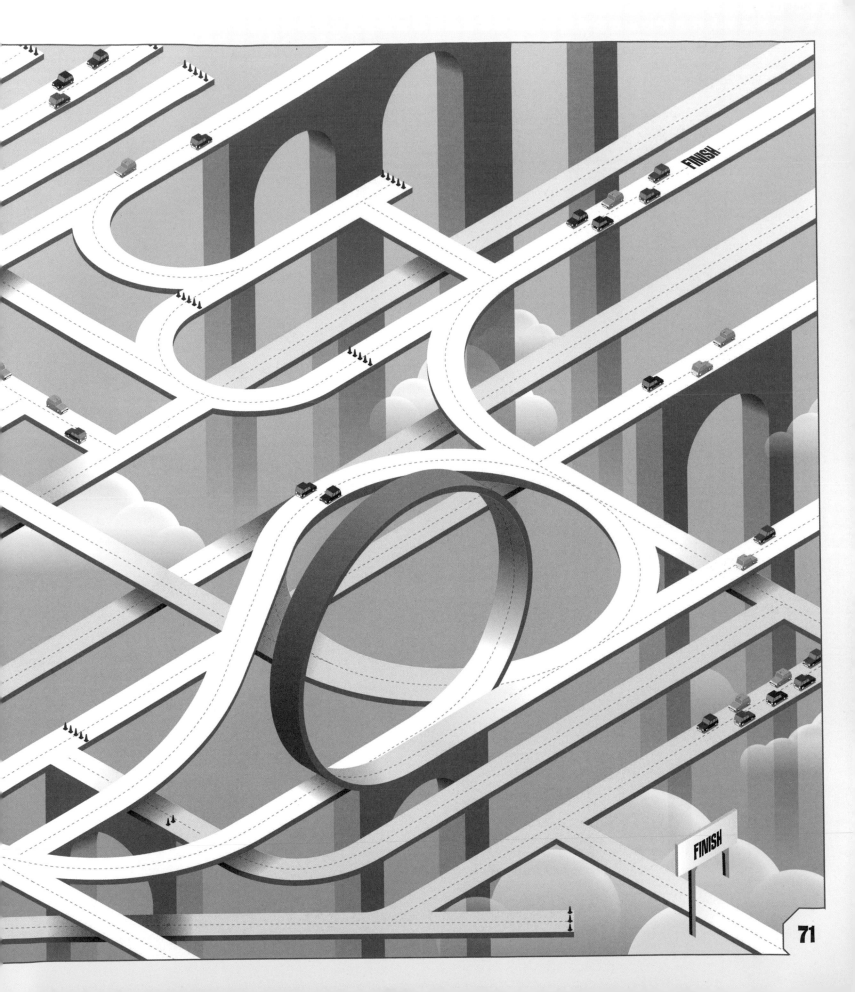

FINISH

FINISH

MINI GOLF

Play each hole in turn,
without retracing your route.

START

FINISH

72

THE RUBY TALISMAN

Trace a line to the magic ruby and the talisman will make you invisible.

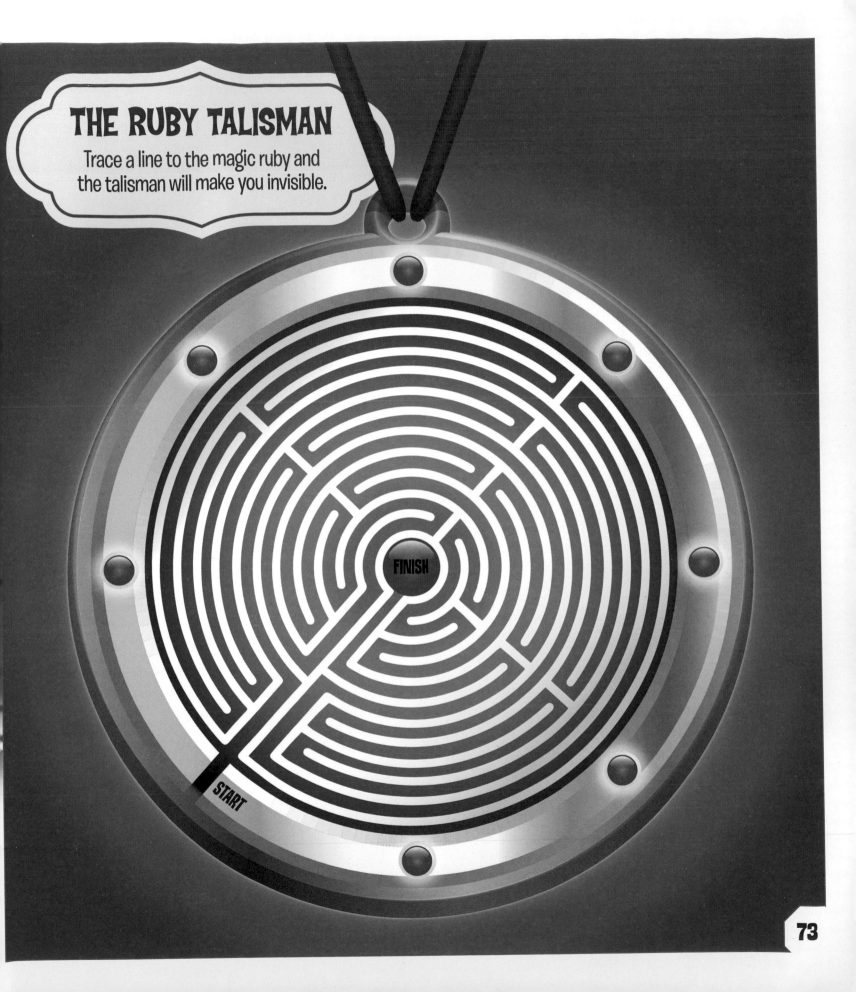

FINISH

START

Don't Drink!

START

Freaky Faucets

Which wheel needs tightening to put a stop to the dripping faucet?

A   B   C   D   E

FAREWELL TOUR

Take in the view from all four flag towers one last time before you leave.

START

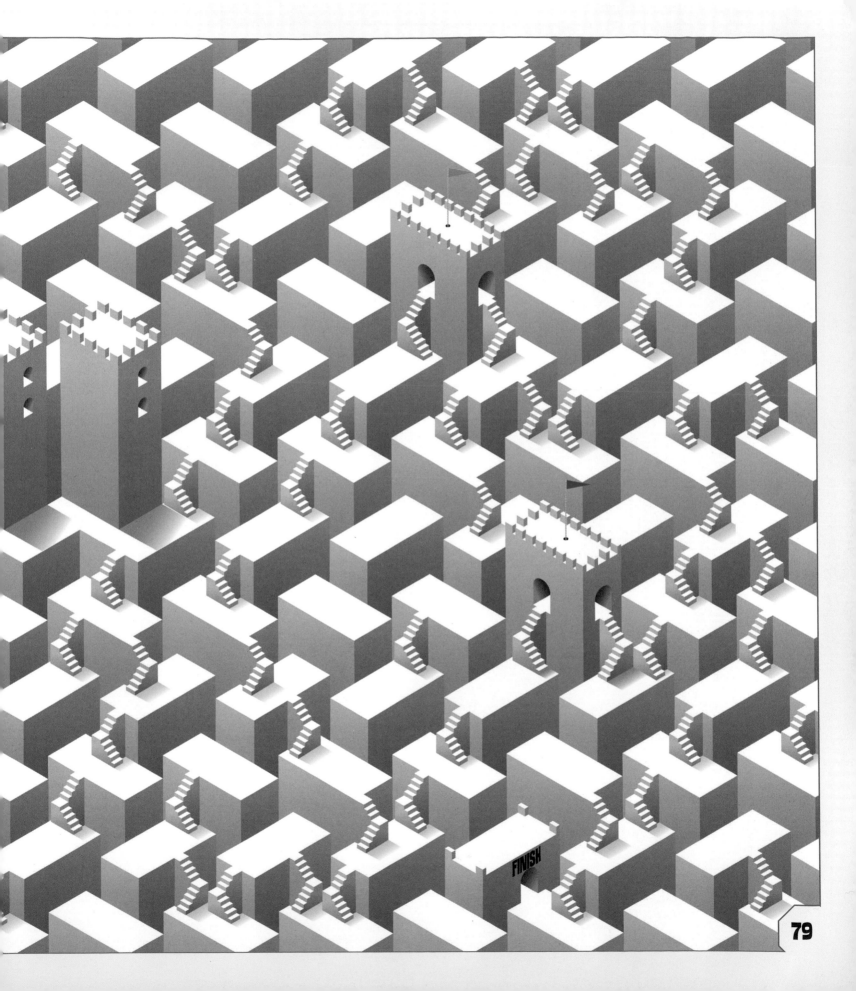

FINISH

ROOM 13

Your room is ready, but you'll need to dodge the ghosts to get there.

FINISH

START

START

START

ROOM WITHOUT A VIEW

It's your first day at the office,
but where exactly is your office?

FINISH

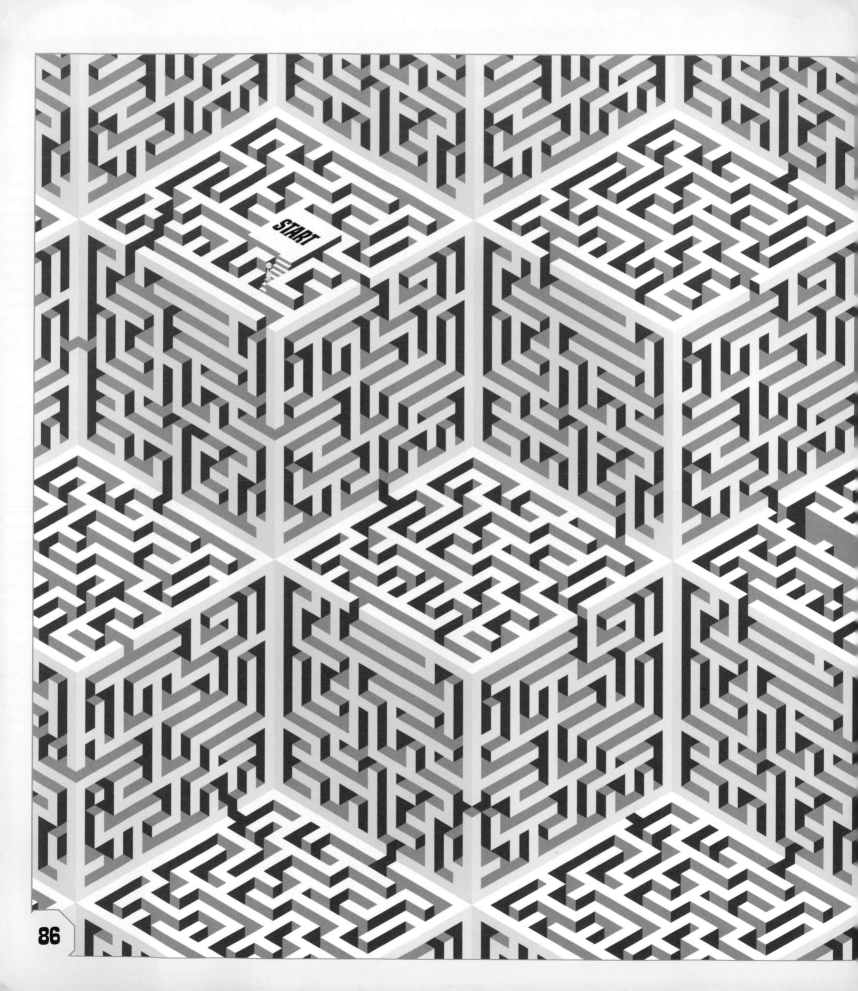

START

JOURNEY'S END

The end is in sight, but now you've got to get there...

FINISH

SOLUTIONS

Page 4

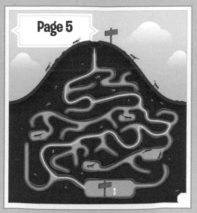

Page 5

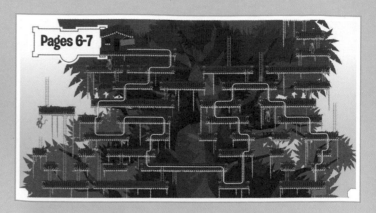

Pages 6-7

Page 8

Page 9

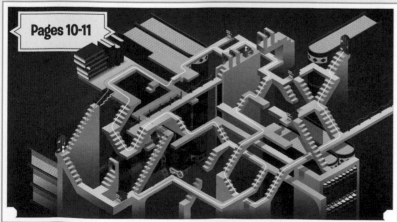

Pages 10-11

Page 12

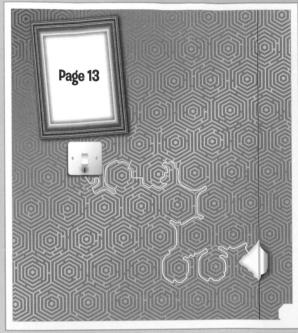

Page 13

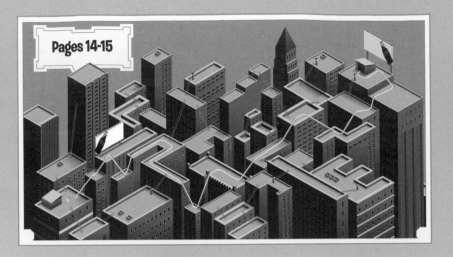

Pages 14-15

Page 16

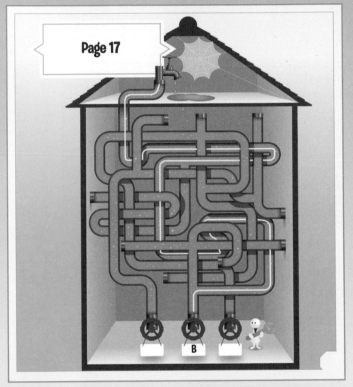

Page 17

Pages 18-19

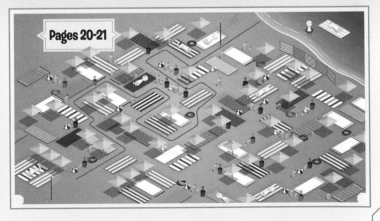

Pages 20-21

Page 22

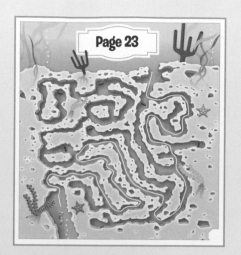

Page 23

Page 24

Pages 26-27

Page 25

Page 28

Page 29

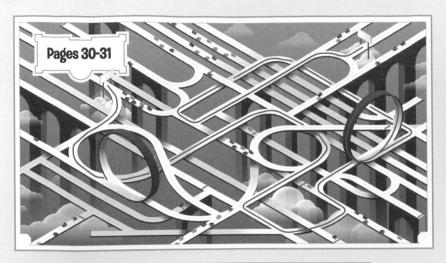

Pages 30-31

Page 32

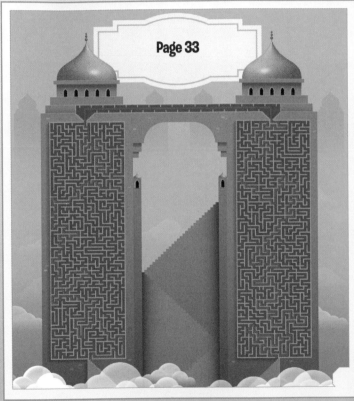

Page 33

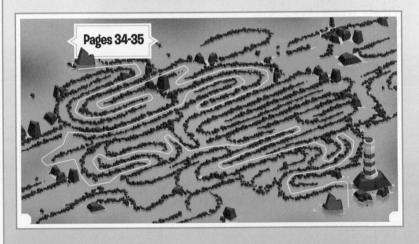

Pages 34-35

Pages 38-39

Pages 36-37

Page 40

Pages 42-43

Page 41

Pages 44-45

Page 46

Page 47

Pages 48-49

Page 50

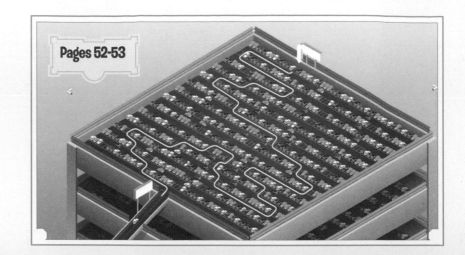

Pages 52-53

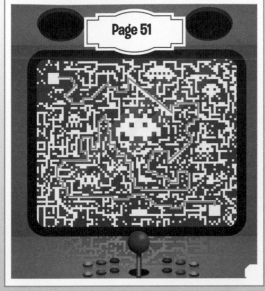

Page 51

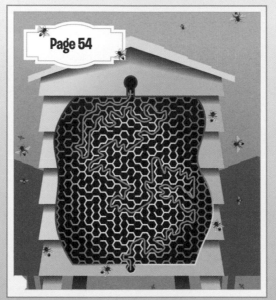

Page 54

Page 55

1 2 3 4 Pages 56-57

Page 58

Page 59

Pages 60-61

Page 62

Page 63

Pages 64-65

Pages 66-67

Pages 68-69

Pages 70-71

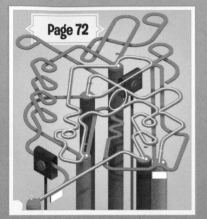
Page 72

Page 73

Pages 74-75

Page 76

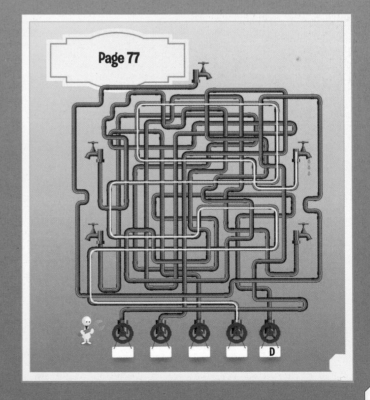
Page 77

Pages 78-79

Pages 80-81

Pages 82-83

Page 85

Page 84

Pages 86-87